The Island Art Association, Inc.

presents

ACKNOWLEDGEMENTS

ISLAND ART ASSOCIATION

Co-Edited by
Kay Vaughan-Bartram and Diana Tyson

Cover Design by
Susi Sax and Eliza Holliday

Graphic Design by
Chris Hamilton

Art Photography by
William Raser

IAA Book Committee
Carol Beck
Sue Hutchinson
Casey Matthews
Roger Moore
Susi Sax
Milt Shirley
Michael Spicer

Printed in China

TABLE OF CONTENTS

Forward 6
Introduction 7
Sandra Pinchback Barwick 9
Pam Bennett. 10
Gary Arseneau 11
Kay Vaughan-Bartram 12
Floyd I. Atkinson. 13
Sandra Baker-Hinton 14
Mary B. Borshard 15
Ruth G. Carden 16
Janice Currie. 17
Lou Coker. 18
Mike Clemens 19
Melba A. Craven 20
Sharon Badenoch. 21
Paul N. Massing 22
Elizabeth Dion 23
Theresa Daily 24
Mikolean Morgan Longacre 25
Armand Gilanyi. 26
Barbara Fuller 27
Don McCurry. 28
Dolly Buck 29
Patricia H. Hooks 30
Chris Hamilton 31
Maryalice LeDuc-Lenmark 32
Sue Hutchinson 33
Christina Long 34
Emily Howard 35
Mari. 36
Marilyn Evans Eflein 37
Kay W. Guess. 38
Casey Matthews 39
Anne Mottayaw. 40
Pat Noonan. 41
Carol Winner 42

Carrie McCannell 43
Ronnie Melnick 44
Norma Jean McLeod 45
Shirley Sykes Bracken 46
Barbara C. Martin 47
Beverly Monahan 48
Louise Mozena 49
M. Lynette Holmes 50
Carol Beck 51
Henry Cook 52
Emylee McBrearty 53
Diane Hamburg 54
Joann S. Speas 55
Gloria Adams 56
Georganna Mullis 57
Candace Fasano 58
Karen A. McFadyen 59
Milt Shirley 60
Bill Raser 61
Susan (Susi) R. Sax 62
L. Ray Pigg 63
Michael Spicer 64
Harvey Sibley 65
Melva Smith-Richman 66
Roger Moore 67
Marlene Strobach 68
Diana Tyson 69
John Thompson 70
Robin Tondra 71
Winston Wiant 72
Michael Van Horn 73
Eileen Shannon Moore 74
Blair Strain 75
Jane Wilson 76
Gretchen Williams 77
Peggy Stanton 78
Artist Information 80

FOREWORD

Join the creative community of artists on Amelia Island and Nassau County as they explore their visions of what was, is, and might yet be. Many of the featured artists are members of the non-profit Island Art Association, publishers of this book. Works of these artists, as well as others, can be seen in our gallery or in one of the other galleries throughout the region, making Amelia Island a major visual arts destination in northeast Florida.

The Island Art Association was inspired by a gathering of like-minded artists in the early 1970's who met to paint at the Atlantic Avenue Recreation Center while exhibiting at the generously donated office of one of our local attorneys. Several rented gallery spaces later on Fernandina Beach's Centre Street led to the eventual purchase of our current gallery on North Second Street.

As to Amelia Island's place in the history of artistic expression, human artifacts have been discovered dating back 4,000 years. Shards of pottery made from a unique clay found only at the mouth of the St. Johns River and decorated with a distinctive design are on display at our local museum and in nearby Jacksonville, Florida.

Artifacts dating from the mid-16th Century illuminate the fierce struggles that resulted in the eight flags that would eventually fly over Amelia Island's 13.5 mile stretch of ocean-side paradise. The first artist of record to visit our area was Jacques le Moyne, who did so at the request of Catherine de Medici, queen of France. The Flemish engraver-jeweler, Theodore de Bry, later created the etchings of the Florida First Coast that would give Europeans one of their first views of the New World.

What made Amelia Island so desirable was the fact that nature blessed us with the deepest natural harbor on North America's coast prior to dredging. Trade goods arrived from around the world. Naturalists like William Bartram and John James Audubon immortalized our heritage in words and sketches.

The late 19th Century brought Amelia Island a Golden Age of Tourism that inspired visitors to preserve their memories with sketches and photographs. We invite our 21st Century visitors to follow in these Victorian footsteps and visit our gallery. We hope Artists of Amelia entices you to explore the many different visions we offer.

Ron Kurtz
Amelia Island Author and Lecturer

INTRODUCTION

Welcome to <u>Artists of Amelia</u>! Each page of this beautiful collection of art, created by Amelia Island and Nassau County artists, invites you to enjoy and be inspired by the diversity, originality, and thoughtfulness of our local arts community. Each artist presents one of their original art works along with a personal message offering you an intimate view of their process, feelings, thoughts, and ideas as they create their art. And, as you identify your favorites, I invite you to use the contact information located in the back section of the book to talk with them, visit their studios, see other pieces in their collections, and purchase their work for your home and office.

The natural beauty of northeast Florida has attracted many talented artists from around the world and across the nation, creating a vibrant and diverse community of both newcomers and homegrown artists in all sorts of creative endeavors: theatre, music, writing, painting, weaving, fiber, pottery, photography, glass and jewelry-making, and sculpture. Amelia Island proudly boasts of many art galleries and studios with new ones opening all the time, a variety of theatre groups, and first class musical presentations throughout the year. We are truly an arts community and are glad you are interested in being a part.

The Island Art Association (IAA), an all volunteer, non-profit organization, offers just one of the galleries located on the island. We chose to publish this book as a fundraiser for our IAA building fund in which we are planning to build a new, spacious, light-filled, modern gallery and classroom space. Diana Tyson and Kay Bartram conceived of this book; an artists' book that would allow our association members and nonmembers an opportunity to display their work and to express their appreciation for the natural beauty of this area.

IAA's humble beginnings started in the 1970's when several artists met to paint together in a local recreation center. Through the years, the group grew and relocated to several studio and gallery spaces along Centre Street and eventually moved to our current home at 18 North 2nd Street in Fernandina Beach, and onto the internet at www.islandart.org.

Not only has our organization changed locations and grown in the number of artists involved, but also, our mission and outreach in the community has grown by leaps and bounds. Some of our current community projects for the arts include:

- "Kids in the Park" classes taught by our artist members at no cost to the participating families.
- $300 donations made to every public school art teacher in Nassau County each year to purchase art supplies. Over the past 10 years we've donated over $18,000.
- College scholarships awarded to graduating Nassau County High School seniors who win a juried art competition. IAA has contributed $50,000 to these talented students over the past 30 years.
- Free arts and crafts classes for senior citizens at the local Council on Aging.
- Juried art shows open to everyone in Nassau County offering recognition and cash prizes in bimonthly shows throughout the year.
- 6000 hours volunteered annually, organizing and managing the arts and crafts portion of the Annual Isle of Eight Flags Shrimp Festival which attracts over 100,000 visitors to Amelia Island each year since 1976.

As you can see, the arts are alive and growing on Amelia Island and you are an important part of what allows artists to flourish in our community. Thank you for supporting our work by purchasing this book and please consider purchasing copies as gifts for friends and family to help us spread the word about <u>Artists of Amelia</u>.

Roger Moore, President 2004-2006
Island Art Association, Inc.

"Nanny's Goin' Fishin'"

Sandra Pinchback-Barwick

"Nanny's Goin' Fishin'" is a watercolor that was created in the way I most often work in this medium and I feel expresses my passion for watercolor. When I began the painting, I put a few pencil lines on the paper indicating areas for sky, water & dunes. There was no preliminary sketch and no preconceived idea of what I was going to paint. Just a desire to get on the paper with some wonderful washes, indicating the sky, water and dune shapes. Just a playful beginning.

I began to think dunes…with impressions of plant life, sea oats, etc. My final expression or thought came from memories as a child fishing, thus the figures en route to a fun filled day with anticipation of things to come.

"Pelican Touchdown" is a one of kind stained glass panel designed and made by the artist. The panel was made by combining several different glass techniques. Traditional stained glass painting was incorporated on the wings, beak and body of the pelican to add extra details. The splash in the water was created by tack-fusing glass pieces together to make the splash look more realistic. Rich Youghogheny stipple glass was chosen for the water not only for the beautiful colorations but for the texture it imparts. The black water glass inside border was chosen for its wonderful reflective quality, and is adorned with a hand-blown Blenko rondel.

32/34

ARSONEAU ©'99

Edition of 34, Printed in 1999 IMP (IMP means printed by the artist's own hand)

Lithography is an original creative medium where an artist draws on a stone, plate or mylar and each image printed by the artist and/or under their direction and approval is an original lithograph.

"9 x 12"

"untitled" "original" (stone) lithograph

Gary Arseneau

Kay Vaughan-Bartram · "Solitude" · oil · 9" x 12" · Private collection, Chicago, IL

Living on a southern coastal marsh gives me the opportunity to see its colors change from moment to moment, hour to hour. The longer I'm here my passion for capturing the moods and beauty of coastal Southeast Georgia & northeast Florida has gone from the eye of the camera to the flow of the artist's brush. The tides and marshes are never the same. The most calming time for me is right after a rain when the landscape is misty and quietly at peace. Everything is in soft textures and nothing has started to stir. It is a time when all is right with our world and it is forever pulling me back to paint again.

Early one morning, when my children were young, my family and I drove out Heckscher Drive on Jacksonville's north side, looking for a good picnic spot. I turned into the road to Fort George Island and was driving under moss-covered oaks, when a glimpse of water flashing through the trees caught my eye. I pulled through a tiny opening into a clearing where a cove had been almost hidden from view. A grassy bank, a sandy shoreline, and marsh that seemed to go on forever. What a beautiful place for a picnic!

A day of fun for the entire family was soon over, but this special place became the inspiration for one of my first landscape paintings.

Floyd I. Atkinson   "Picnic on Fort George Island"   oil & acrylic   30" x 40

13

"Midday Dune Vista" depicts the brilliant effects of the bright noontime sunshine as it reflects on the dunes of the beach in its blinding "sunglasses required" way. The use of the very wet, acrylic colors as they are encouraged to flow together further creates the illusion of the shimmer of the hot sun as it gives new life to the beach and dune grasses in early summer. The feeling, rather than a detailed rendering, is what is achieved in this large walk into format painting. The influence of a career of watercolor painting shows its results in this painting technique with its combination of opaque acrylic paint using water to make the colors become very aqueous.

30" x 40"

acrylic

"Midday Dune Vista"

Sandra Baker-Hinton

Mary B. Borshard   "Resurrection Fern"   watercolor   18" x 24"   Private collection, Amelia Island, FL

This painting, "Resurrection Fern", was created after carefully executing a good abstract design. Gradually, with the addition of several watercolor applications and some planned collaged overlays, the painting was completed. I took it to the Waterwheel Art Enterprises for matting and framing and was asked what the title was. I had no idea. I had been too engrossed in its creation to even think about that. Alan Ralph, owner of the Waterwheel, suggested 'Resurrection Fern'. "That is perfect," I exclaimed. Alan replied, "Mary, that's what it is!" This piece was included in my exhibit at the Cummer Museum in Jacksonville, FL and was the public's favorite over all my other paintings there.

Ruth G. Carden   "Banishing Melancholy"   fiber art collage   20" x 30"

Small pieces of fabric serve as my paint and whole cloth is my canvas. Putting bits of fabric together to form a whole is much like life. Each of us plays many roles that fit together to make up a total being, just as the bits of fabric make my collages.

During the late summer of 2005, my concerns for the victims of the war in Iraq, hurricanes and other disasters had led to a feeling of despair and hopelessness. Making this piece encouraged me to explore different materials and methods and to focus on dreams, good memories and relationships, and most of all, hope.

Janice Currie

Coleridge defines poetry as… "the power of giving (the) interest of novelty by (the) modifying colors of imagination". "Color Happy" is an effort through painting to create poetry. Using watercolor as a medium produces surprising fusions. The arrangement of colors, using complimentary colors, contrast and a bold warm red was primary to the basic structure. When water is involved in the process, it causes an imagination of its own. Water adds the variety.

Artists, including composers, writers and speakers, reflect their own personality and preference through their works. This particular painting became a true challenge when a diagonal stripe was added. Many trial stripes appeared and disappeared. Initially, some were solid, some blank, some were run on sentences and some simply did not rhyme. Finally, the right stroke, for me, appeared.

26" x 32"

watercolor

"Pineapples"

Lou Coker

The richness I admire comes from nature. At an outdoor market in Switzerland I saw these pineapples, surrounded by flowers and I sanctioned their esthetic by evoking a presence by means of a shadow and the whole by means of a figment. This evokes my affinity, if you like, to our own eighteenth-century painters, with whom I recognize a close kinship with their sensitivity and technique.

After retiring in 2004, I moved to Fernandina Beach and decided to become serious about "throwing pots". Although throwing lids for bowls that fit and altering wheel thrown items is challenging, as an amateur potter, I obtain personal satisfaction from attempting to accomplish these tasks.

In regard to the three items on this page, the plate and lidded bowl were both thrown on a pottery wheel. The casserole was wheel thrown, then altered and assembled by hand. All three items have the same glaze and were fired to cone 10.

pottery

Mike Clemens

transparent watercolor

"Cosmos"

Melba A. Craven

I love flowers and love to paint the beauty of them. This painting is a transparent watercolor on Arches 140 lb. paper. A tight close-up of the flower was used to show structure, pattern & detail. The dark values were painted first and then shapes were lifted to give interest in this area. The dark values add drama which give the light values their translucence, while the crisp edges of the flowers contrast with the soft shapes suggested in the background.

The obvious challenge was to keep the flowers white and still show dimension so they didn't look like dirty flowers.

This painting was inspired by the view in our own backyard. The vast expanse of the salt marsh dotted with pine trees, palms and moss covered oaks is breathtaking as well as peaceful.

A small island surrounded by water is nearby which I chose for my subject. It was a typical hot, humid, steamy Florida day and I tried to convey that in my watercolor. I hope I succeeded.

15" x 18"

watercolor

"Steam Heat"

Sharon Badenoch

20" x 24"

acrylic

"A Knife Splash"

Paul N. Massing

Having studied art as a young man and later working in science and engineering, I developed a personal sensitivity to the "doing" of art. I like to explore the processes of various media to produce a piece. Although "abstract painting" is a personal preference, drawings and paintings from nature and doing portraiture are satisfying experiences in my artist life.

The painting shown here is a small work done in acrylic media with touches of oil pastel and prisma color. It was done in the genre of "Abstract Expressionism", which was an art form mainly in America in the mid-nineteen hundreds and continues to be a painting form today. I have added a splash of white color as an element into the work and used that stroke to title the painting. My abstract paintings are executed in short work sessions so that the work is an expression of color and motion in a spontaneous, energetic manner.

36" x 54"

acrylic

"Earth Plane"

Elizabeth Dion

This painting is a landscape suggestive of many places and, perhaps, no physical place at all. I hope others see it as anywhere their own imagination takes them when they look at it. It is built up with many layers of translucent paint, giving it texture and an ethereal quality of light. It is a process that leaves many opportunities for sparks of intuition and imagination. This painting bridges these two aspects of my work and represents for me a direction in which I wish to continue.

At the time I was working on this piece, I was reading "Isle of Palms" by Dorothea Benton Frank. With the steamy southern atmosphere in the book in mind, this painting called for strong values to express a feeling of warm, bright sunlight with cool, deep shadows.

My objective was to portray an ordinary subject in an unusual way. This was achieved by using an alternate palette for the focal area and minimal local color in the background and shadow areas. By flattening the image plane and using an overall pattern of line and shape, the simple palm fronds became almost geometric and abstract.

By allowing watercolor the freedom to express itself, you just may be surprised what comes off the tip of your brush!

Theresa Daily   "Isle of Palms"   watercolor   36" x 48"

Bronze

"Tommy"

Armand Gilanyi

This work is a bronze portrait of my son, Thomas, when he was four years old. It is a work that embodies the love of a father for his son. Even as time passes, for a parent their children always remain children. Bronze is a timeless medium, perfect for capturing a parent's image of their child, an image that never ages even as time passes.

Barbara Fuller

"Resolutions, New Beginnings"

watercolor

The inspiration for this painting was my thoughts and hopes for the New Year. The amaryllis and the branches of pussy willows represent rebirth and thoughts of springtime. The stacked books to be read and the photos of friends and family to be put into an album, allude to my tendency to procrastinate and a desire to change that habit. The patriotic symbols hint at the year of the presidential election. The paisley fabric design, a pattern derived from the Near East, suggests that in these troubled times we are all of the same cloth no matter how much we try to deny that fact.

This painting just flowed from me, and I am happy to say, won me "The Best of Show" prize.

photography

"Cormorants on Submerged Dugout Canoe"

Don McCurry

I was cruising through the Everglades on an overcast day. With very little contrast, there wasn't much to photograph until I stumbled on two cormorants with almost mirror image reflections in the still water. It wasn't until I had the photograph developed that I realized they were standing on a waterlogged, partially submerged dugout canoe.

The beauty and tranquility of the beach has always been a source of inspiration for me. I love the scents and sounds of the waves, the dunes, and the graceful sea oats, and looking and listening to all the shore birds. I hope to share the peace and serenity with the viewer.

Dolly Buck   "Path Between the Dunes"   watercolor   14" x 20"

During a trip to Maine and Nova Scotia I was charmed by the magnificent coastal scenery. I became especially fascinated with the colorful boats both docked and anchored out in the waters. It seemed at every turn there were row-boats, either serenely resting or bobbing, in the inlets, bays and marinas. To me, there is a mystique about empty, working boats with their rigs, oars, and colorful, lobster buoys waiting for someone to take them out.

"Dynamic Duo" is a portrayal of two rowboats carelessly jammed into a slip. I particularly enjoyed using the strong, primary colors which are predominant in many of my nautical scenes. I took pleasure in painting the water which transitioned from dark and still in the foreground to rippled and sunlit in the background. This painting won several awards for me in northeast Florida.

Patricia H. Hooks   "Dynamic Duo"   watercolor   15" x 30"   Private collection, Jacksonville, FL

30

As a native Floridian, I have always lived near water. This image portrays the coastal lifestyle as I see it, calm, laid back, and inspiring.

Chris Hamilton "Still Waters" pencil 23" x 30"

Maryalice LeDuc-Lenmark

This very beautiful egret was, for several years, a frequent visitor to the docks and picnic tables around Walkers' Landing. For reasons unknown, he was affectionately named "Walter" by near-by residents. Walter would descend unannounced, without fanfare or circling, and perch almost motionless for long periods of time. He would often allow me, and camera, to come within inches of where he was resting. Walter has not been seen at the Landing for several months, so I am especially grateful to him for permitting this photograph. (Photograph taken with 35mm camera without the use of a telephoto lens.)

In 1932, Gus Gerbing (1900-1984) created Gerbing's Gardens devoted at first to the production of both azaleas and camellias and later to camellias alone. Gerbing's objective was to create a formal garden on fifteen acres along the Amelia River. He moved tons of material from the river bottom to develop a moist, nutrient laden soil where his plants could thrive. Above the Azalea Terrace, Gerbing created a camellia windbreak 800 feet long planted entirely with Sarah Frost camellias. An adjoining 1800 foot walk was surrounded by azaleas, dogwood and flame vine hedges.

Today, the area where the gardens once flourished along Gerbing Road, many varieties of azaleas, camellias, spirea and wisteria still bloom during February and March. This was painted to capture and preserve a small portion of Fernandina Beach.

watercolor

"Azalea Terrace, Gerbing's Gardens"

Sue Hutchinson

33

Christina Long

"Technocracy"

acrylic

30" x 40"

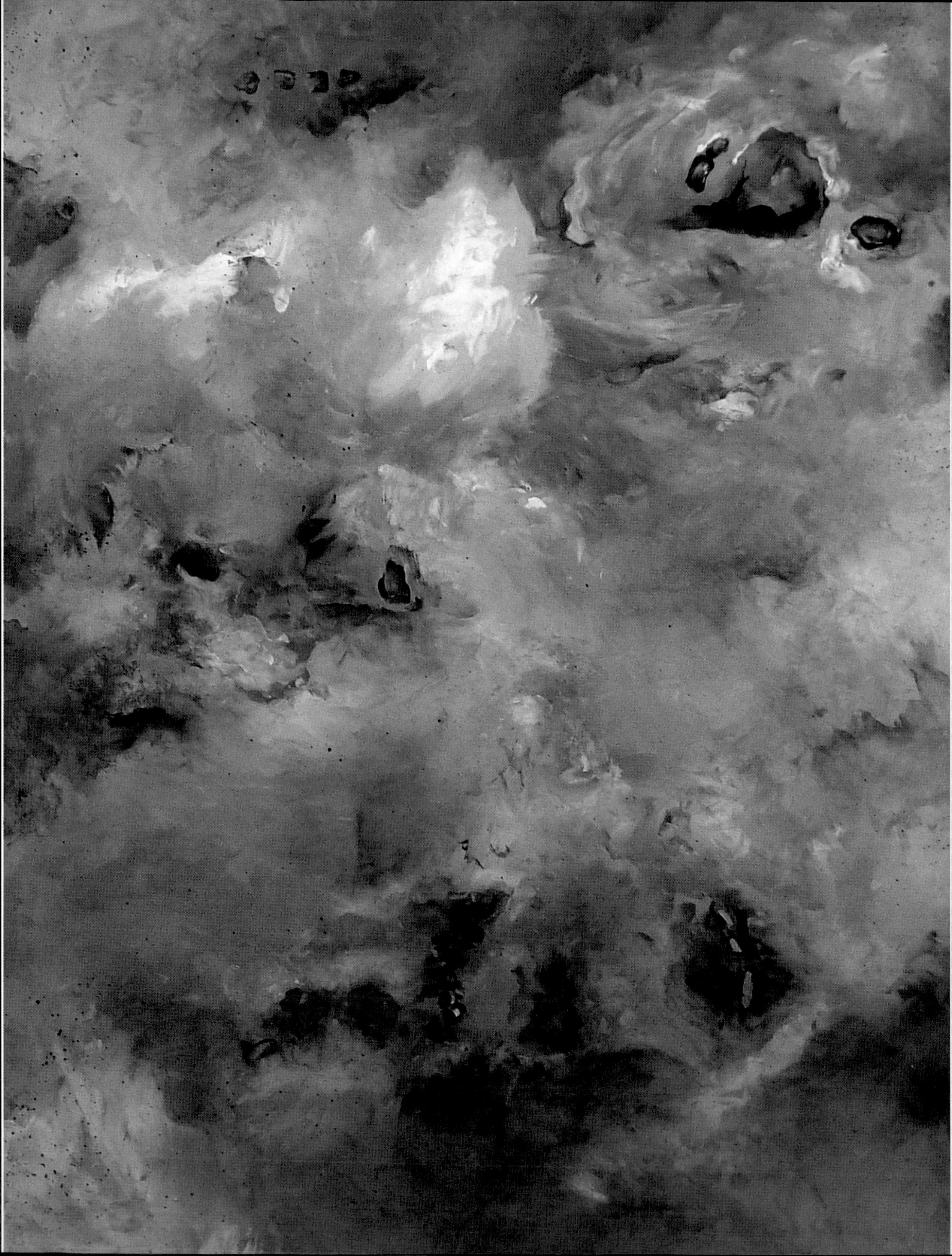

This paint
by the broken price
it involved finger p

My direction as an artist has been to capture a moment in time. It could be early morning, late evening, sunrise, sunset, rain, wind or fog. When creating this painting I wanted to show the mystery and excitement of a night scene, with a full moon giving magic to everything it touched.

36" x 40"

acrylic

"Amelia's Moon Light Magic"

Emily Howard

35

40" x 40"

oil

"...and then, do you know what she told me?"

Mari

This painting is an expressionistic and somewhat eskewed interpretation of what is beautiful and intriguing in my life and environment. It invites you to come into a colorful world of dream fantasy and real life spin that holds subtle innuendo in the form of a "narrative" painting.

The stage is set. The viewers complete the scenario as they choose.

The high tide of summer beckons; a flag awaits a time honored place; a hastily chalked message proclaims the distraction from its reign; the siren call of the ocean and warm sand sing its song. Sultry breezes blow gently through the open door as palm shadows splash about the walls and floor. Calmly aloof, a vigilant green-eyed feline surveys her domain. This idyllic tableau sets the mood for celebrating the "everyday" of island life. This painting was the front cover for the Talking Phone Book 2004-2005 in the Fernandina Beach area.

Being a native of Florida, the ocean, marshlands, waterfront and local characters are my inspiration; perhaps because they are ingrained into my psyche. I strive to capture the essence, the one moment in time that all who live near the sea have seen, tasted, or felt. Once I capture "that moment" my goal has been achieved.

Marilyn Evans Eflein   "Summer Daze"   watercolor   11" x 15"

37

This particular piece was inspired during a boat ride in and out of the tidal creeks around the marshlands of Amelia Island. I saw not only the egrets wading and feeding, I also saw the pink spoonbill at it's nesting site on the marsh islands. My fascination with the great egret was exemplified by the first time I saw one in flight. In flight or at rest, this bird's magnificent grace is totally enchanting. This painting expresses my personal vision of this quiet and peaceful scene.

17" x 24"

oil

"Egrets on Amelia Island"

Kay W. Guess

     My current body of work is primarily abstract, mixed media painting, and is a constant discourse between intuitive and non-objective. The process is a marriage of layered acrylic paint, medium, gesso, charcoal, glazes, washes, handmade paper, collage, tissue, spit, and oil, on canvas. Gestural sparks of interest are often added with vine charcoal, oil sticks, and collage or spiced text. A typical piece is then sealed and buffed with wax.

     My intention is to create layers of information through my technique, and combine the bold structure of graphic design with spontaneous painting. I am not a tortured artist, nor are my struggles unique; it comes down to what I consider essential characters in my work. The relationship between colors, humor, energy, and lack of intimidation are the sources I draw from.

Anne Mottayaw   "Grand Avenue Vista"   watercolor   32" x 40"

Cumberland Island has always had a special place in the hearts of our family. We were privileged many years ago to have Lucy Ferguson take our family on a tour. For years, we rode down historic Grand Avenue where the stately oaks bend their arms overhead welcoming and embracing us. I felt I wanted to capture their beauty.

I began the watercolor working from my photographs. I usually paint 16 x 20's, but felt I could not do justice with anything but a much larger piece. Classes on depth perception helped me realize I was not using enough dark tones to capture the depth of the forest while still emphasizing the oyster shell road itself. I was challenged to capture the sunlit, blue sky overhead, filtering through the lacy, leaf canopy, allowing occasional spotlights on the growth below.

ISLAND ART ASSOCIATION
A R T
Island Art Association Gallery
2nd Street North

in order to cherish its beauty, I decided to capture the rapture of this beautiful gift.

"My Cymbidium"   acrylic   20" x 24"

Pat Noonan

I love a good story and draw from mythology, history, biography, fables and my own personal stories. I approach a new painting as if observing a dream: not judging or questioning, simply trusting that it will emerge in its own good time. I play, pushing a good composition and letting color speak its mind, keeping the voice that says "you can't do that", at bay, remembering van Gogh saying, "It is our obligation as artists to disregard public opinion". I feel that my current work is the most honest of my career; viewers sense and appreciate this, often connecting on a spiritual level with common stories and human experiences.

I'm happiest in my Florida studio, listening to my muse, writing stories in paint.

"Bindy Sue"

12" x 12"

acrylic

Carrie McCannell

Dogs are only in our lives a short time, but what an impact they can make! I've often been moved to capture the personality of dogs I've known and loved in portrait as a loving way of freezing them in time forever. It all starts with the eyes, where all dogs show their personality. Bindy Sue, the subject of this piece, has a cat-like sophistication and slow, demure movements. She stares at you with almost human eyes as if she wishes she could understand each word you say to her.

All my dog paintings have a bright yellow background which seems to offset all dogs with a regal glow. I like to use thick, acrylic paint and continue the piece even on the sides of the canvas to give the image texture and dimension. As a finishing touch, I often use one of the dog's own ID tags on the piece.

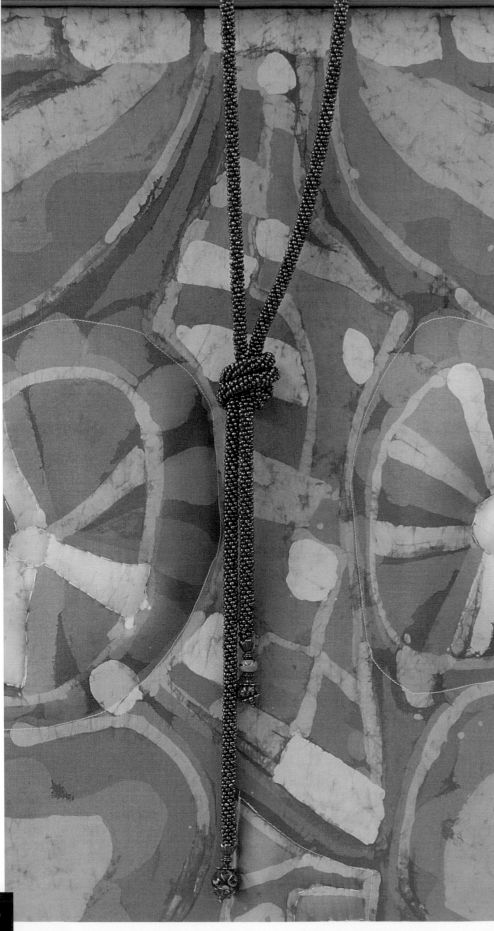

Having been an artist for the past 35 years I have found that I enjoy using small components to form an object. I began my art career as an abstract painter and then discovered beads. I love the many textures, shapes, colors and finishes. I have used beads to embellish textiles as well as for jewelry making. This piece was made using copper-colored, Czech, glass, seed beads called "Charlottes" due to the facet on one side of the bead. I used copper components to enhance the lamp-worked beads given to me by a friend who made them. The small beads work together to make a fluid form that is pleasing to the touch and comfortable to wear.

photography

"Catch of the Day"

Norma Jean McLeod

Waking up each morning only a stone's throw from Lofton Creek has afforded me the pleasure of observing almost every species of Florida water birds. This Osprey, commonly known as a fish hawk, swooped down and caught his striped mullet before my eyes. He perched in my moss-laden, giant, water oak to enjoy.

This work was painted in the early morning. The interesting quality of the light along with this man's unique means of commuting to work became the focal point of the piece. I like both painting and photographing shrimp boats, not only because they are interesting, but because they are becoming a thing of the past on Amelia Island.

22" x 30"

watercolor

"Commute to Work"

Shirley Sykes Bracken

Light reflections have interested me for years. At Rocamadour, a medieval pilgrimage fortress clinging to the cliffs overlooking the River Alzou, in the mountains of southern France, the reflected, late afternoon light, reflected, creates a full spectrum of colors.

This painting continues exploring light reflecting, primarily from natural stone surfaces. Here, the tiles of village roofs, and accompanying terraces, walls, and gardens, interspersed with native vegetation and rock outcroppings, offer a wide range of absorbed and reflected light.

The light itself doesn't appear as color. Only through reflections are we aware of the chromatic range and the potential for mood expressions. I wanted to capture the almost magical, brilliantly saturated colors of a summer moment brimming with sunlight.

Barbara C. Martin   "Rocamadour sur la Dordogne, France"   acrylic   30" x 40"   Private collection, Amelia Island, FL

My husband and I visited Saint Paul de Vence while on vacation. It is one of the most beautiful villages in all of Provence. The beauty of the surrounding area, quality of life, and exceptional light has inspired numerous famous artists, painters, writers and poets. On our walks through the maze of narrow and picturesque streets of the village we discovered magnificent, centuries-old stone facades and enjoyed the floral gardens, ancient fountains, porches and wonderful windows.

It is difficult not to feel like creating in this wonderful atmosphere. I love painting scenes from all over the world. Some real, some imagined. In all of my paintings I start with a little reality and add a little imagination.

Amelia Island marshes are intriguing and inspiring because of the ever changing light. The medium of transparent watercolor lends itself well to portraying patterns of light and shadow on the marsh grasses, trees, and tidal water.

"High Tide" is a composite of various scenes that I see on the south end of the island. I want to portray the golden, morning light on the marsh in early spring. The viewer's eye roams throughout the painting following the white of the birds and patterns of reflections in the water and on the trees. Amelia Island's special light creates interesting patterns not only on the marshes, palmettos and water, but also on the historic buildings of Fernandina Beach.

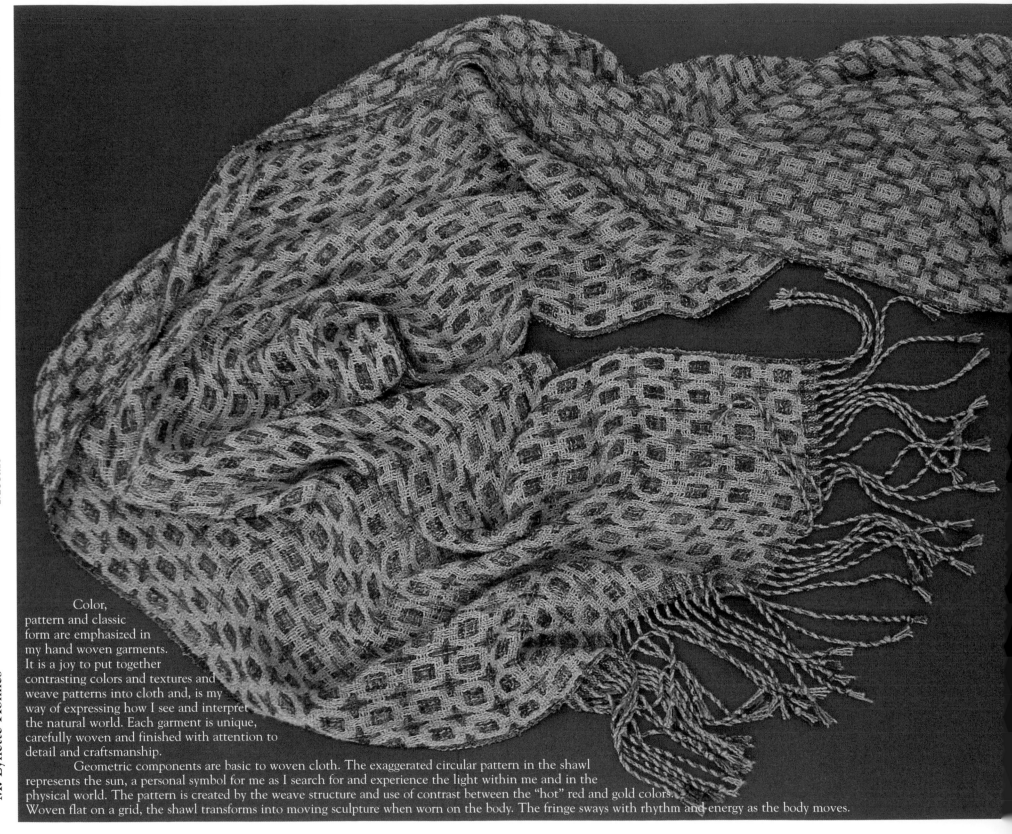

fiber shawl

"Mosaic"

M. Lynette Holmes

Color, pattern and classic form are emphasized in my hand woven garments. It is a joy to put together contrasting colors and textures and weave patterns into cloth and, is my way of expressing how I see and interpret the natural world. Each garment is unique, carefully woven and finished with attention to detail and craftsmanship.

Geometric components are basic to woven cloth. The exaggerated circular pattern in the shawl represents the sun, a personal symbol for me as I search for and experience the light within me and in the physical world. The pattern is created by the weave structure and use of contrast between the "hot" red and gold colors. Woven flat on a grid, the shawl transforms into moving sculpture when worn on the body. The fringe sways with rhythm and energy as the body moves.

I come to my art through my background as an intuition teacher. As a result, my intuitive abstracts are not about *seeing* a familiar object but instead about feeling. Feeling freedom, freshness, hope, and fun to name a few. I painted "Splash" after a day at the beach with family and friends. I wanted it to feel joyful, with colors and light literally vibrating off the canvas just as they did on the ocean. As with most of my paintings, it is my hope that "Splash" will encourage you to reclaim the child-like ease of getting lost in play and remind you to bring into your daily life a sense of wonder and delight.

12" x 12"

acrylic / watercolor

"Splash"

Carol Beck

"Fishing Buddies" 18" x 24" acrylic

Henry Cook

In my approach to a work, I either visually or mentally "see" something that I wish to express on canvas or paper. In this case, I started with a shrimp boat, which to me displays a kind of excitement about life in Fernandina. And then I did numerous "thumb-nails" to create focal points and then let the story formulate the colors that compliment the work.

The thought came to me to let the subjects (the boy, pelican and one of the shrimp boat workers) have a common thread, fishing. The docks, fog, and the early morning became supporting subjects. The pelican approaching the "caught" fish sort of adds a touch of humor which I include in many of my works.

Whether painting a still life or landscape, I love painting en plein air. This particular painting was done in the spring when the sunshine was calling me to "come out", but the wind was just too gusty. So, instead, I set up the still life in the window of my studio overlooking the same area. I painted it over a period of 3 days, painting at the same time each day so that the light would be consistent. Making the green leaves of the grapes stand out against the green shrubbery showing through the window became quite a challenge. When I felt like giving up and scraping the whole thing down, I cleaned my brushes and put my work aside. The next day the inspiration, which had created the set up, was back enabling me to make it work.

Emylee McBrearty   "Light From the Window"   oil   20" x 24"

Right after discovering the joy and meditative aspects of printing real leaves, my eye caught the beautiful heart shaped leaves of a vine covering a weathered fence in Fernandina. I recently discovered that this vine is actually non-native to Florida and is considered invasive. I guess the old saying "Take the bad with the good" applies even to leaves.

This quilted art piece is a mixture of techniques. I dyed white cotton fabric and then printed the leaves using acrylic fabric paint. Once the fabric backing, batting, and decorated front fabric were layered, free motion, machine-quilting textured the surface. Separate quilted leaves were highlighted using oil stick paints and attached to the top along with machine-made lace leaves. I made yarn cords to weave between the leaves as the stems of the vine; finally, beading further textured the piece.

The world is full of beautiful surprises. As the tour group from the Mint Museums of Charlotte turned the corner to enjoy our last dinner in Milan, there appeared this magnificent structure. I have painted incredible architecture and incredible personalities from all over the world, and one never runs out of subject matter. Alone, this façade presents the possibility of several other paintings.

Working in graphite and watercolor I work in an impressionistic genre and I love what I do.

"Palazzo – Milano" watercolor/graphite 22" x 30"

Joann S. Speas

55

watercolor

"Heart Of Palm"

Gloria Adams

"Heart of Palm" began as a project for a workshop I attended. The instructions were to look deeper into the form, search for the positive and negative shapes and color values. I awoke really early one morning to begin my work. With coffee in hand, I surveyed the black and white picture the instructor had given me. Feeling there must be more to this picture, my eyes moved to my outside window where a beautiful palm stood right in my own back yard. Seeing the early morning light hit somewhere around the middle of the majestic tree, I could see it very clearly now. Color, shape and its "heart" suddenly appeared.

24" x 40"

acrylic

"Palm Alone"

Georganna Mullis

    I call this island on which I have lived for the past 36 years my home. We all have our favorite places and reasons for being on Amelia Island, mine are simple enough. The painting vistas never let me down, no matter where or when I look, or what the weather.

    This painting has come from all the influences in my life, both visual and spiritual, that compel me to paint. My fascination is with color and movement that is ever-changing here depending on the time of day or season of the year. The stately palm tree says so simply "island living". In the right sunlight, color changes from dull grays and greens to vibrant reds, yellows and oranges with purple, violet, and blue shadows. Every one of my paintings is the sum of all I have seen and felt as I live my life.

Delicate patterns in nature like the honeycomb are simple and elegant yet amazing in their ability to support life. Visually, this pattern can also be pushed to look like a chain link fence. Dualities and contradictions including the formal concerns of abstraction and representation are interesting subject matter that can, poetically, convey everyday life. It is an exhilarating journey to combine and reinterpret the languages of painting; fitting them together like puzzles, in order to express something relevant to both our inner and outer worlds.

48" x 36"

oil & mixed media

"Honey Moon"

Candace Fasano

58

Private collection, Fernandina Beach, FL

30" x 40"

oil

"The Opening # II"

Karen A. McFadyen

This painting was inspired by a gift. A fellow artist gave me the beautiful amaryllis to celebrate an opening for an exhibit of my work, as the show included several of my paintings of the Florida landscape. I was intrigued by the contrast between the living plant and my painted tributes to nature's bounty. I decided to include the bow as a symbol of the gift—God's gift of nature's beauty and the thoughtful gift of friendship. I made several drawings of the subject at the gallery as studies for the painting. I completed the painting (the second in a series) in my studio in the spring of 2000.

30" x 40"

oil

"Marsh at Early Morning"

Milt Shirley

Milt Shirley

The marshes are never the same. They change by the season, the month, the day and often by the hour. I try to capture these changes brought on by the thunderstorms, sunrises, sunsets or simply days-so-clear, you can see forever. I am a marsh painter, that's what I do.

As a professional photographer I photograph just about anything: products, advertising, events, portraits, and fine art images. But the photography I find most fascinating is aerial photography of Amelia Island. The south end is perfectly clear and the island blurs into the misty distance of the north end with the port and mills, and then fades to St. Mary's and Cumberland Island. What I like the most in this image is the halo effect on the slight curvature of the earth, almost as if you were viewing Amelia Island from outer space.

"Amelia from Above"   photography

Bill Raser

61

"Freddie of Fernandina in the Forest" watercolor 30" x 40"

Susan (Susi) R. Sax

There are words and words, but the joy I get when I do a watercolor is beyond description. When I fuse glass or create glass etching I still get the adrenaline rush as I did when I first started my art back when I was a little girl. Enjoy!!!

This is a view from the dining room of the Golf Club of Amelia Island showing the eighteenth green and fairway. This vantage point from the pleasant environment of the Club, documents the perspiration-filled toil of the golfer under the hot, Florida sun in the pursuit of the ever-elusive wild fowl: the Birdie and the Eagle.

L. Ray Pigg   "...but it's hot out there!"   watercolor   18" x 24"

I love Amelia Island's rich history and culture, historical neighborhoods, wildlife and plants, wetlands and seascapes, and glorious sunsets and moonrises; all providing broad brushstrokes of paint on a canvas rich in beauty. As a photographer, I am especially interested in observing and capturing the interactions between light and our surroundings.

In this photograph, the Fernandina marina provides a backdrop in the late afternoon as boats return with their catch for the day. Always on the lookout for an easy meal, eager pelicans fly-in and amble up as fishermen clean their fish and toss away scraps; wings flap and contenders fight in frequent tugs-of-war over their meal. The boats in the background provide a hint of the history of the area when pirates actually worked the coastal waters around Amelia Island.

"The Pelicans of Amelia"

Michael Spicer

The patron for this painting served in the Pacific; thus the sea color and oriental motifs. As contemporary art, it builds on art of the past, shuns realism, and employs pattern, color, texture and composition to create interest in an intelligent, open-minded viewer.

"Sailing the Sulu Sea"

acrylic ink, sumatran anolyn dye

23" x 30"

Harvey Sibley

This woven tapestry is wool weft (surface) woven on cotton warp.

"My Friend"

This is my friend Walter, a Great Egret. He lives at Walker's Landing on Amelia Island. Since Walker's Landing has a fishermen's boat ramp, he hangs out here and helps the returning fishermen dispose of their unused bait. The fishermen are his friends and I am too. As soon as my lunch is on the picnic table, there's Walter. Will I share my sandwich? Of course. I don't offer him the bread any more since he only goes for the chicken salad filling. In turn, Walter will pose for me and my camera. He likes the late afternoon sun. "It makes for a better picture of me," he says. This bird knows his photography.

Roger Moore

watercolor

"Iris II"

Marlene Strobach

What inspires an artist? For me, the inspiration for this painting was Georgia O'Keefe's home. As I was meandering through the grounds of the inn in Abiquiu, New Mexico and contemplating Georgia's work, I came upon these irises growing randomly. I was filled with desire to paint them. Inspiration comes from deep within and produces the best work. I like to call it "soul". And I was ready.

My purpose was to capture the sunlight shining upon the iris from above, which I created by leaving white paper showing through the painting. Then I created diffused light in the otherwise contrasting background and leaves by allowing colors to run together and rubbing out some areas to create mystery.

The ocean has many moods. In this particular moment it is lazy, with long, slow, smooth waves lapping onto the beach leaving wet sand with each receding wave. I wanted to capture the essence of the atmosphere with soft light bouncing off the clouds and the reflected light glistening through the water and onto the sand. It was not my goal to recreate the scene, but the emotion. Luminous drifting clouds were developed by glazing technique with acrylic paint. Let the sand invite you to take your shoes off. Let the next wave wash gently over your feet and the fresh, salt air fill your lungs. Time stops and you are caught in the moment, captured as the title suggests.

Diana Tyson   "Captured by Light"   acrylic   30" x 40"   Private collection, Amelia Island, FL

"Main Street Bridge, July 4, 2004"

acrylic

24" x 31"

John Thompson

For a couple of years now I have been exploring nocturnal paintings through my Plein Air paintings.

The entire color spectrum changes at night. The sun sets and the air changes and cools, creating colors not usually painted. When adding the fireworks to the night, the celebration of light, charges the air with vibrant colors of red and orange against the dark blue and purple blacks. What better way to spend the evening than capturing the light of the Nocturne.

Robin Tondra   "Fur Up My Nose"   acrylic   11" x 14"   Private collection, Rhode Isla

71

This painting was inspired by the use of the palette knife. I have always been taken by the style of impressionistic art and have worked through the years to relate this through the paintings I have created.

The use of the palette knife has been a long-term goal of mine and I think I have finally captured the concept. I slowly learned the way to move the knife around the canvas, capturing the full effect and bringing the subject matter to the surface. Nothing else mattered when painting on this canvas; the movement, thick paint and light source all came together, creating this work of art!

This long-abandoned South Georgia tobacco barn is of a structural style referred to as "vernacular architecture"; that is, a design which is strongly identified with a particular region. Usually constructed of the most readily available materials, barns of this general type are found wherever flue-cured tobacco is grown.

I've used acrylic on 300# D'Arches Rough watercolor paper, detailing the work with ink and pencil. The flexibility of this medium lends itself to my style, which has been described by reviewers as "documentary" in its approach.

acrylic

"South Georgia Drive-In"

Michael Van Horn

My beach and landscapes manage to capture the essence of what I'm painting. My scenes offer airy images of sand dunes, the sea, and shore birds flying in a peach and blue washed sky. In this painting, I used an opaque background with signature details layered over warm, ocean-inspired pastel colors.

For 25 years I was an exhibiter at major art shows across the United States but now I concentrate on Eileen's Arts and Antiques and the Island Art Association.

I prefer to paint from life. People of all ages, colors and situations inspire me. And, the human face fascinates me.

My work is intense, bright, colorful and dramatic. Although I frequently use pastels on mid to dark color papers, I also paint with oils, acrylics, mixed media and collage. The vivid color and value contrast in the subject matter is inspired by the beauty of nature and character in the faces around me.

BLAIR

pastel

"Hannah"

Blair Strain

75

23" x 20"

watercolor

"Western Sunflowers"

Jane Wilson

This watercolor was inspired by living in Las Vegas, NV. The sunflowers grew and flourished in the harsh, desert climate and they seemed so joyous to be alive and thriving that I just had to try and capture their beauty. I hope you enjoy my efforts to immortalize some of the beauty of the Mojave Desert.

Watercolors are my obsession. To capture and preserve a moment of history, a favorite subject, composition, color, or even a moment of intrigue fascinates me. I hate to be bored or depressed. The Amelia Island homes excite me with stories behind the structures and the people who inhabit them for their time on earth. The Four Sisters were easy to paint but the one in particular fascinated me and I wanted to bring it into a balance with the others. Plein Air painting allows me to paint small renditions and return to my studio if I feel the painting needs to be larger scale.

watercolor

"The Sisters on Seventh"

Gretchen Williams

"Mother of all People"

Peggy Stanton

prismacolor

The "Little Pilgrim" is reading scripture in the fields of a remarkable village named Medjugorje, nestled in the hills of Bosnia-Herzegovina. When Bosnia was part of the former Yugoslavia, Medjugorje, high in the mountains, was so remote, it was not even a dot on the map. In 1981, six young people living in the village, claimed visitations from the Mother of Jesus, the Blessed Virgin Mary. Miraculous sightings and healings were reported and suddenly the world discovered Medjugorje. Over 22 million people have pilgrimaged to this tiny hamlet in search of the kind of peace exhibited by this "Little Pilgrim" and as one pastor put it, "they come home different people".

Island Art Association, Inc.
18 North 2nd Street
Fernandina Beach, Florida 32035-1251
904.261.7020
islandart@net-magic.net
www.islandart.org

Cover Lettering and Layout By: Eliza Holliday ~ Eliza Lettering Design, Fernandina Beach, FL 904.277.4834

Book Design and Layout By: Chris Hamilton ~ Hamilton Press, Fernandina Beach, FL 904.261.6510

Artists' Information

Gloria Adams 56
904.277.6610
Amelia Island, FL
gloadams1@aol.com

Gary Arseneau 11
904.321.0021
Fernandina Beach, FL
gwarseneau@hotmail.com

Floyd I. Atkinson 13
904.225.0504
Yulee, FL

Sharon Badenoch 21
904.261.1192
Amelia Island, FL
badenochj@bellsouth.net

Kay Vaughan-Bartram 12
904.261.8823 H
904.753.0537 C
Amelia Island, FL
kaybartram@comcast.net
www.kaybartramstudios.com

Sandra Pinchback-Barwick . . . 9
904.321.2793 H
904.415.6575 C
904.321.0833 W
Fernandina Beach, FL
barwicksb@aol.com

Carol Beck 51
904.491.0250
Fernandina Beach, FL
selfdiscovery@bellsouth.net
www.carolbeck.net

Pam Bennett 10
904.491.4778
Fernandina Beach, FL
stainedglassbypam@yahoo.com

Mary B. Borshard 15
904.261.8385
Fernandina Beach, FL
mborshard@net-magic.net

Shirley Sykes Bracken 46
Amelia Island, FL
rickshirley68@earthlink.net
www.artistoriginals.net

Dolly Buck 29
904.261.2082
Amelia Island, FL
benbuckjr@msn.com

Ruth G. Carden 16
904.277.1562 H
904.557.1185 C
Amelia Island, FL
ragcarden@aol.com

Mike Clemens 19
904.206.4466
Fernandina Beach, FL
mclem5fam@comcast.net

Lou Coker 18
904.261.4660
Fernandina Beach, FL

Henry Cook 52
904.945.6363
hw_cook@msn.com

Melba A. Craven 20
904.261.8429
Fernandina Beach, FL
bobcrav@aol.com

Janice Currie 17
904.277.8153
Fernandina Beach, FL
megcurrie-7@webtv.net

Theresa Daily 24
Fernandina Beach, FL
dailydouble.2@earthlink.net

Elizabeth Dion 23
904.321.1686
Fernandina Beach, FL
lizdion@bellsouth.net

Marilyn Evans Eflein 37
Fernandina Beach, FL
meflein@hotmail.com

Candace Fasano 58
904.261.0243 H
904.583.4402 C
Fernandina Beach, FL
clfasano@comcast.net

Barbara Fuller 27
904.277.1553
Amelia Island, FL
dickfuller@mindspring.com

Armand Gilanyi 26
904.491.6303
Fernandina Beach, FL
wallartgallery@hotmail.com

Kay W. Guess 38
904.261.9537 H
904.753.3400 C
Fernandina Beach, FL
kblossom99@aol.com

Diane Hamburg 54
904.261.9229
Fernandina Beach, FL
jimndihamburg@net-magic.net

Chris Hamilton 31
904.261.6510
Fernandina Beach, FL
Chris@HamiltonPress.biz

Sandra Baker-Hinton 14
904.491.7986 H
904.557.1195 C
Fernandina Beach, FL
sbh@sandrabaker-hinton.com

Eliza Holliday . . . . Cover
904.277.4834
Fernandina Beach, FL
eliza@letterist.com

M. Lynette Holmes 50
904.261.6810 H
904.557.1187 C
Fernandina Beach, FL
holmeslyn@aol.com

Patricia H. Hooks 30
904.277.2597
Fernandina Beach, FL
path11@comcast.net

Emily Howard 35
904.261.5008
Fernandina Beach, FL

Sue Hutchinson 33
904.321.2524
Fernandina Beach, FL
iosme@aol.com

Maryalice LeDuc-Lenmark . . 32
904.261-3235
Fernandina Beach, FL
mledlen@aol.com

Christina Long 34
904.261.9880
Fernandina Beach, FL
info@citrona.net

Mikolean Morgan Longacre. . 25
904.491.8537
Fernandina Beach, FL
tmpromark@aol.com

Mari 36
904.261.6707
Fernandina Beach, FL
mariart@bellsouth.net

Barbara C. Martin 47
904.261.7020
Amelia Island, FL
bcbcmartin@aol.com

Paul N. Massing. 22
904.321.0738
Fernandina Beach, FL
paulmassing1@bellsouth.net

Casey Matthews. 39
904.491.1426 H
904.556.1119 C
Fernandina Beach, FL
caseysartstudio@aol.com

Emylee McBrearty 53
904.491.0369
Fernandina Beach, FL
jandemcb@aol.com

Carrie McCannell. 43
904.261.5831 H
813.786.4654 C
Fernandina Beach, FL
csmccannell@yahoo.com

Don McCurry 28
904.261.7111
Amelia Island, FL
mccurryor@aol.com

Karen A. McFadyen. 59
904.261.3665
Fernandina Beach, FL
mcfadyens@bellsouth.net

Norma Jean McLeod 45
904.225.0878
Fernandina Beach, FL
njmcleod@bellsouth.net

Ronnie Melnick 44
904.261.9381 H
Fernandina Beach, FL
pchee72@bellsouth.net

Beverly Monahan 48
904.277.2091 H
904.477.0416 C
Fernandina Beach, FL
bevmoods@aol.com

Eileen Shannon Moore 74
904.556.5722
Fernandina Beach, FL
emoore@fdn.com

Roger Moore. 67
904.277.4403
Amelia Island, FL
rogmoore@bellsouth.net

Anne Mottayaw. 40
904.261.4722
Fernandina Beach, FL
jcmottayaw@bellsouth.net

Louise Mozena. 49
904.261.7132
Amelia Island, FL
dcmozena@worldnet.att.net

Georganna Mullis 57
904.556.5724 C
904.261.4899 I I
Fernandina Beach, FL
ga1artist@yahoo.com

Pat Noonan. 41
215.292.5084
Amelia Island, FL

L. Ray Pigg 63
904.261.4563
Amelia Island, FL
lrpigg@comcast.net

Bill Raser 61
904.261.0813
Fernandina Beach, FL
wjraser@comcast.net

Melva Smith-Richman 66
904.321.4323 H
904.477.0866 C
Amelia Island, FL
melvasr@bellsouth.net

Susan R. Sax 62
904.321.1330 H
904.583.3842 C
Fernandina Beach, FL
sussid5555@aol.com

Milt Shirley. 60
904.225.1938
Fernandina Beach, FL
mands123@roverusa.com

Harvey Sibley. 65
904.277.2879
Amelia Island, FL
harveysibleyart@aol.com

Joann S. Speas 55
904.321.0903
Amelia Island, FL

Michael Spicer 64
904.491.8658
Fernandina Beach, FL
michaelspicer@bellsouth.net
www.michaelspicer.net

Peggy Stanton 78
904.206.4140 H
440.477.0700 C
Amelia Island, FL
peggystanton@aol.com

Blair Strain 75
904.277.8670
Fernandina Beach, FL
bblairstrain@aol.com

Marlene Strobach. 68
904.277.4486
Amelia Island, FL
estrobach@comcast.net

John Thompson 70
904.613.1741 C
Yulee, FL
jthomp944s@bellsouth.net

Robin Tondra 71
904.277.2979 H
404.277.7669 C
Fernandina Beach, FL
robin@crazydogart.com

Diana Tyson 69
912.449.0132 H
Blackshear, GA
dptyson@atc.cc

Michael Van Horn 73
904.261.9763
Fernandina Beach, FL
llp@net-magic.net

Winston Wiant 72
Amelia Island, FL
eocrawford@bellsouth.net

Gretchen Williams. 77
904.491.3171
Fernandina Beach, FL
gretchwi@aol.com

Jane Wilson. 76
904.261.8097
Fernandina Beach, FL
bluebonnet@bellsouth.net

Carol Winner 42
904.583.4676
Fernandina Beach. FL
rothrockwinner@aol.com